The
Best Poems
Ever

SCHOLASTIC CLASSICS

the Best Poems ever

a collection of poetry's greatest voices

Edited by Edric S. Mesmer

SCHOLASTIC INC.

New York Toronto London Auckland Sydney
Mexico City New Delhi Hong Kong Buenos Aires

ISBN 0-439-29674-9

Permissions are located on page 72.

12 11 10 9 8 7 6 5 4 3 2 1   1 2 3 4 5 6/0

Printed in the U.S.A.   01

First Scholastic printing, September 2001

TABLE OF CONTENTS

BLESSING THE BOATS

Lucille Clifton

(at St. Mary's)

may the tide
that is entering even now
the lip of our understanding
carry you out
beyond the face of fear
may you kiss
the wind then turn from it
certain that it will
love your back   may you
open your eyes to water
water waving forever
and may you in your innocence
sail through this to that

THE AUTHOR TO HER BOOK

Anne Bradstreet

Thou ill-formed offspring of my feeble brain,
Who after birth didst by my side remain,
Till snatched from thence by friends, less wise than true,
Who thee abroad, exposed to public view,
Made thee in rags, halting to th' press to trudge,
Where errors were not lessened (all may judge).
At thy return my blushing was not small,
My rambling brat (in print) should mother call,
I cast thee by as one unfit for light,
Thy visage was so irksome in my sight;
Yet being mine own, at length affection would
Thy blemishes amend, if so I could:
I washed thy face, but more defects I saw,
And rubbing off a spot still made a flaw.
I stretched thy joints to make thee even feet,
Yet still thou run'st more hobbling than is meet;
In better dress to trim thee was my mind,
But nought save homespun cloth i' th' house I find.
In this array 'mongst vulgars may'st thou roam.
In critic's hands beware thou dost not come,
And take thy way where yet thou art not known;
If for thy father asked, say thou hadst none;
And for thy mother, she alas is poor,
Which caused her thus to send thee out of door.

WHEN GREAT DOGS FIGHT

Melvin B. Tolson

He came from a dead-end world of under breed,
A mongrel in his look and in his deed.

His head sagged lower than his spine, his jaws
Spooned wretchedly, his timid little claws
Were gnarls. A fear lurked in his rheumy eye
When dwarfing pedigrees paraded by.

Often he saw the bulldog, arrogant and grim,
Beside the formidable mastiff; and sight of them
Devouring chunks of meat with juices red
Needled pangs of hunger in his belly and head.

Sometimes he whimpered at the ponderous gate
Until the regal growls shook the estate;
Then he would scurry up the avenue,
Singeing the hedges with his buttercup hue.

The spool of luckless days unwound, and then
The izzard cur, accurst of dogs and men,
Heard yelps of rage beyond the iron fence
And saw the jaws and claws of violence.

He padded through the gate that leaned ajar,
Maneuvered toward the slashing arcs of war,
Then pounced upon the bone; and winging feet
Bore him into the refuge of the street.

A sphinx haunts every age and every zone:
When great dogs fight, the small dog gets a bone.

from TO A SKYLARK

Percy Bysshe Shelley

Hail to thee, blithe spirit!
   Bird thou never wert,
That from heaven, or near it,
   Pourest thy full heart
   In profuse strains of unpremeditated art.

Higher still and higher
   From the earth thou springest
Like a cloud of fire;
   The blue deep thou wingest,
   And singing still dost soar, and soaring ever singest.

In the golden lightning
   Of the setting sun,
O'er which clouds are brightening,
   Thou dost float and run
   Like an unbodied joy whose race is just begun.

SONNET 130

William Shakespeare

My mistress' eyes are nothing like the sun;
Coral is far more red than her lips' red;
If snow be white, why then her breasts are dun;
If hairs be wires, black wires grow on her head.
I have seen roses damasked, red and white,
But no such roses see I in her cheeks,
And in some perfumes is there more delight
Than in the breath that from my mistress reeks.
I love to hear her speak, yet well I know
That music hath a far more pleasing sound.
I grant I never saw a goddess go;
My mistress when she walks treads on the ground.
    And yet, by heaven, I think my love as rare
    As any she belied with false compare.

A RED HAT

Gertrude Stein

A dark grey, a very dark grey, a quite dark grey is monstrous ordinarily, it is so monstrous because there is no red in it. If red is in everything it is not necessary. Is that not an argument for any use of it and even so is there any place that is better, is there any place that has so much stretched out.

EXILE'S LETTER

Rihaku (Li Po)

To So-Kin of Rakuyo, ancient friend, Chancellor of Gen.
Now I remember that you built me a special tavern
By the south side of the bridge at Ten-Shin.
With yellow gold and white jewels, we paid for songs
    and laughter
And we were drunk for month on month, forgetting the
    kings and princes.
Intelligent men came drifting in from the sea and from
    the west border,
And with them, and with you especially
There was nothing at cross purpose,
And they made nothing of sea-crossing or of mountain-
    crossing,
If only they could be of that fellowship,
And we all spoke out our hearts and minds, and without
    regret.
And then I was sent off to South Wei,
    smothered in laurel groves,
And you to the north of Raku-hoku,
Till we had nothing but thoughts and memories in
    common.
And then, when separation had come to its worst,
We met, and travelled into Sen-Go,

8

Through all the thirty-six folds of the turning and
        twisting waters,
Into a valley of the thousand bright flowers,
That was the first valley;
And into ten thousand valleys full of voices and pine-
        winds.
And with silver harness and reins of gold,
Out came the East of Kan foreman and his company.
And there came also the "True man" of Shi-yo to meet me,
Playing on a jewelled mouth-organ.
In the storied houses of San-Ko they gave us more
        Sennin music,
Many instruments, like the sound of young phoenix
        broods.
The foreman of Kan Chu, drunk, danced
        because his long sleeves wouldn't keep still
With that music playing,
And I, wrapped in brocade, went to sleep with my head
        on his lap,
And my spirit so high it was all over the heavens,
And before the end of the day we were scattered like
        stars, or rain.
I had to be off to So, far away over the waters,
You back to your river-bridge.
And your father, who was brave as a leopard,
Was governor in Hei Shu, and put down the barbarian
        rabble.

And one May he had you send for me,
    despite the long distance.
And what with broken wheels and so on, I won't say it
    wasn't hard going,
Over roads twisted like sheep's guts.
And I was still going, late in the year,
    in the cutting wind from the North,
And thinking how little you cared for the cost,
    and you caring enough to pay it.
And what a reception:
Red jade cups, food well set on a blue jewelled table,
And I was drunk, and had no thought of returning.
And you would walk out with me to the western corner
    of the castle,
To the dynastic temple, with water about it clear as blue
    jade,
With boats floating, and the sound of mouth-organs and
    drums,
With ripples like dragon-scales, going grass green on the
    water,
Pleasure lasting, with courtezans, going and coming
    without hindrance,
With the willow flakes falling like snow,
And the vermilioned girls getting drunk about sunset,
And the water, a hundred feet deep, reflecting green
    eyebrows
— Eyebrows painted green are a fine sight in young
    moonlight,

Gracefully painted —
And the girls singing back at each other,
Dancing in transparent brocade,
And the wind lifting the song, and interrupting it,
Tossing it up under the clouds.
And all this comes to an end.
And is not again to be met with.
I went up to the court for examination,
Tried Layu's luck, offered the Choyo song,
And got no promotion,
And went back to the East Mountains
White-headed.
And once again, later, we met at the South bridge-head.
And then the crowd broke up, you went north to San
    palace,
And if you ask how I regret that parting:
It is like the flowers falling at Spring's end
Confused, whirled in a tangle.
What is the use of talking, and there is no end of talking,
There is no end of things in the heart.
I call in the boy,
Have him sit on his knees here
To seal this,
And send it a thousand miles, thinking.

translated by Ezra Pound

(UNTITLED)

Aphra Behn

Not to sigh and to be tender,
   Not to talk and prattle Love,
Is a Life no good can render,
   And insipidly does move:
Unconcern do's Life destroy,
   Which, without Love, can know no Joy.

Life, without adoring Beauty,
   Will be useless all the day;
Love's a part of Human Duty,
   And 'tis Pleasure to obey.
In vain the Gods did Life bestow,
   Where kinder Love has nought to do.

What is Life, but soft desires,
   And that Soul, that is not made
To entertain what Love inspires,
   Oh thou dull immortal Shade?
Thou'dst better part with Flesh and Blood,
   Than be, where Life's not understood.

IN A STATION OF THE METRO

Ezra Pound

The apparition of these faces in the crowd;
Petals on a wet, black bough.

ODE TO ENCHANTED LIGHT

Pablo Neruda

Under the trees light
has dropped from the top of the sky,
light
like a green
latticework of branches,
shining
on every leaf,
drifting down like clean
white sand.

A cicada sends
its sawing song
high into the empty air.

The world is
a glass overflowing
with water.

translated by Ken Krabbenhoft

LIFE IN A LOVE

Robert Browning

> Escape me?
> Never —
> Beloved!
While I am I, and you are you,
>   So long as the world contains us both,
>   Me the loving and you the loth,
While the one eludes, must the other pursue.
My life is a fault at last, I fear:
>   It seems too much like a fate, indeed
>   Though I do my best I shall scarce succeed.
But what if I fail of my purpose here?
It is but to keep the nerves at strain,
>   To dry one's eyes and laugh at a fall,
And baffled, get up and begin again, —
>   So the chase takes up one's life, that's all.
While, look but once from your farthest bound
>   At me so deep in the dust and dark,
No sooner the old hope drops to ground
>   Than a new one, straight to the self-same mark,
>   I shape me —
>   Ever
>   Removed!

THE RAVEN

Edgar Allan Poe

Once upon a midnight dreary, while I pondered, weak
and weary,
Over many a quaint and curious volume of forgotten
lore —
While I nodded, nearly napping, suddenly there came a
tapping,
As of some one gently rapping, rapping at my chamber
door —
"'Tis some visitor," I muttered, "tapping at my chamber
door —
Only this and nothing more."

Ah, distinctly I remember it was in the bleak December;
And each separate dying ember wrought its ghost upon
the floor.
Eagerly I wished the morrow; — vainly I had sought to
borrow
From my books surcease of sorrow — sorrow for the lost
Lenore —
For the rare and radiant maiden whom the angels name
Lenore —
Nameless *here* for evermore.

And the silken, sad, uncertain rustling of each purple
    curtain
Thrilled me — filled me with fantastic terrors never felt
    before;
So that now, to still the beating of my heart, I stood
    repeating
"'Tis some visitor entreating entrance at my chamber
    door —
Some late visitor entreating entrance at my chamber
    door; —
        This it is and nothing more."

Presently my soul grew stronger; hesitating then no
    longer,
"Sir," said I, "or Madam, truly your forgiveness I implore;
But the fact is I was napping, and so gently you came
    rapping,
And so faintly you came tapping, tapping at my
    chamber door,
That I scarce was sure I heard you" — here I opened
    wide the door; —
        Darkness there and nothing more.

Deep into that darkness peering, long I stood there
    wondering, fearing,
Doubting, dreaming dreams no mortal ever dared to
    dream before;

17

But the silence was unbroken, and the stillness gave no
  token,
And the only word there spoken was the whispered
  word, "Lenore?"
This I whispered, and an echo murmured back the word,
  "Lenore!"
  Merely this and nothing more.

Back into the chamber turning, all my soul within me
  burning,
Soon again I heard a tapping somewhat louder than
  before.
"Surely," said I, "surely that is something at my window
  lattice;
Let me see, then, what thereat is, and this mystery
  explore —
Let my heart be still a moment and this mystery
  explore; —
  'Tis the wind and nothing more!"

Open here I flung the shutter, when, with many a flirt
  and flutter,
In there stepped a stately Raven of the saintly days of yore;
Not the least obeisance made he; not a minute stopped
  or stayed he;
But, with mien of lord or lady, perched above my
  chamber door —

Perched upon a bust of Pallas just above my chamber
    door —
        Perched, and sat, and nothing more.

Then this ebony bird beguiling my sad fancy into smiling,
By the grave and stern decorum of the countenance it
    wore,
"Though thy crest be shorn and shaven, thou," I said,
    "art sure no craven,
Ghastly grim and ancient Raven wandering from the
    Nightly shore —
Tell me what thy lordly name is on the Night's
    Plutonian shore!"
        Quoth the Raven "Nevermore."

Much I marvelled this ungainly fowl to hear discourse so
    plainly,
Though its answer little meaning — little relevancy bore;
For we cannot help agreeing that no living human being
Ever yet was blessed with seeing bird above his chamber
    door —
Bird or beast upon the sculptured bust above his
    chamber door,
        With such a name as "Nevermore."

But the Raven, sitting lonely on the placid bust, spoke
    only

That one word, as if his soul in that one word he did
    outpour.
Nothing farther then he uttered — not a feather then
    he fluttered —
Till I scarcely more than muttered "Other friends have
    flown before —
On the morrow *he* will leave me, as my Hopes have
    flown before."
        Then the bird said "Nevermore."

Startled at the stillness broken by reply so aptly spoken,
"Doubtless," said I, "what it utters is its only stock and
    store
Caught from some unhappy master whom unmerciful
    Disaster
Followed fast and followed faster till his songs one
    burden bore —
Till the dirges of his Hope that melancholy burden bore
    Of 'Never — nevermore.'"

But the Raven still beguiling my sad fancy into smiling,
Straight I wheeled a cushioned seat in front of bird, and
    bust and door;
Then, upon the velvet sinking, I betook myself to
    linking
Fancy unto fancy, thinking what this ominous bird of
    yore —

What this grim, ungainly, ghastly, gaunt, and ominous
    bird of yore
        Meant in croaking "Nevermore."

This I sat engaged in guessing, but no syllable expressing
To the fowl whose fiery eyes now burned into my
    bosom's core;
This and more I sat divining, with my head at ease
    reclining
On the cushion's velvet lining that the lamp-light
    gloated o'er,
But whose velvet-violet lining with the lamp-light
    gloating o'er,
        She shall press, ah, nevermore!

Then, methought, the air grew denser, perfumed from
    an unseen censer
Swung by seraphim whose foot-falls tinkled on the
    tufted floor.
"Wretch," I cried, "thy God hath lent thee — by these
    angels he hath sent thee
Respite — respite and nepenthe from thy memories of
    Lenore;
Quaff, oh quaff this kind nepenthe and forget this lost
    Lenore!"
        Quoth the Raven "Nevermore."

"Prophet!" said I, "thing of evil! — prophet still, if bird
    or devil! —
Whether Tempter sent, or whether tempest tossed thee
    here ashore,
Desolate yet all undaunted, on this desert land
    enchanted —
On this home by Horror haunted — tell me truly, I
    implore —
Is there — *is* there balm in Gilead? — tell me — tell
    me, I implore!"
        Quoth the Raven "Nevermore."

"Prophet!" said I, "thing of evil! — prophet still, if bird
    or devil!
By that Heaven that bends above us — by that God we
    both adore —
Tell this soul with sorrow laden if, within the distant
    Aidenn,
It shall clasp a sainted maiden whom the angels name
    Lenore —
Clasp a rare and radiant maiden whom the angels name
    Lenore."
        Quoth the Raven "Nevermore."

"Be that word our sign of parting, bird or fiend!" I
    shrieked, upstarting —

"Get thee back into the tempest and the Night's
    Plutonian shore!
Leave no black plume as a token of that lie thy soul
    hath spoken!
Leave my loneliness unbroken! — quit the bust above
    my door!
Take thy beak from out my heart, and take thy form
    from off my door!"
        Quoth the Raven "Nevermore."

And the Raven, never flitting, still is sitting, *still* is
    sitting
On the pallid bust of Pallas just above my chamber door;
And his eyes have all the seeming of a demon's that is
    dreaming,
And the lamp-light o'er him streaming throws his
    shadow on the floor;
And my soul from out that shadow that lies floating on
    the floor
        Shall be lifted — nevermore!

THE POET IS SERVED HER PAPERS

Lorna Dee Cervantes

So tell me about fever dreams,
about the bad checks we scrawl
with our mouths, about destiny
missing last bus to oblivion.

I want to tell lies
to the world and believe it.
Speak easy, speak spoken to,
speak lips opening on a bed of nails.

Hear the creaking of cardboard
in these telling shoes?
The mint of my mind
gaping far out of style?

Hear the milling of angels
on the head of a flea?
My broke blood is sorrel, is a lone
mare, is cashing in her buffalo chips.

As we come to the cul-de-sac
of our heart's slow division
tell me again about true
love's bouquet, paint hummingbird

hearts taped to my page.
Sign me over with XXXs
and *passion*. Seal on the lick
of a phone, my life. And pay.

And pay. And pay.

BUFFALO DUSK

Carl Sandburg

The buffaloes are gone.
And those who saw the buffaloes are gone.
Those who saw the buffaloes by thousands and how they
    pawed the prairie sod into dust with their hoofs,
    their great heads down pawing on in a great pageant
    of dusk,
Those who saw the buffaloes are gone.
And the buffaloes are gone.

ODE ON A GRECIAN URN

John Keats

Thou still unravished bride of quietness,
   Thou foster-child of silence and slow time,
Sylvan historian, who canst thus express
   A flowery tale more sweetly than our rhyme:
What leaf-fringed legend haunts about thy shape
   Of deities or mortals, or of both,
     In Tempe or the dales of Arcady?
   What men or gods are these? What maidens loth?
What mad pursuit? What struggle to escape?
     What pipes and timbrels? What wild ecstasy?

Heard melodies are sweet, but those unheard
   Are sweeter; therefore, ye soft pipes, play on;
Not to the sensual ear, but, more endeared,
   Pipe to the spirit ditties of no tone:
Fair youth, beneath the trees, thou canst not leave
   Thy song, nor ever can those trees be bare;
     Bold Lover, never, never canst thou kiss,
Though winning near the goal — yet, do not grieve;
     She cannot fade, though thou hast not thy bliss,
For ever wilt thou love, and she be fair!

Ah, happy, happy boughs! that cannot shed
    Your leaves, nor ever bid the Spring adieu;
And, happy melodist, unwearièd,
    For ever piping songs for ever new;
More happy love! more happy, happy love!
    For ever warm and still to be enjoyed,
        For ever panting, and for ever young;
All breathing human passion far above,
    That leaves a heart high-sorrowful and cloyed,
        A burning forehead, and a parching tongue.

Who are these coming to the sacrifice?
    To what green altar, O mysterious priest,
Lead'st thou that heifer lowing at the skies,
    And all her silken flanks with garlands drest?
What little town by river or sea shore,
    Or mountain-built with peaceful citadel,
        Is emptied of this folk, this pious morn?
And, little town, thy streets for evermore
    Will silent be; and not a soul to tell
        Why thou art desolate, can e'er return.

O Attic shape! Fair attitude! with brede
    Of marble men and maidens overwrought,
With forest branches and the trodden weed;
    Thou, silent form, dost tease us out of thought
As doth Eternity: Cold Pastoral!

When old age shall this generation waste,
Thou shalt remain, in midst of other woe
Than ours, a friend to man, to whom thou say'st,
Beauty is truth, truth beauty, — that is all
Ye know on earth, and all ye need to know.

THE NIGHT DANCES

Sylvia Plath

A smile fell in the grass.
Irretrievable!

And how will your night dances
Lose themselves. In mathematics?

Such pure leaps and spirals ——
Surely they travel

The world forever, I shall not entirely
Sit emptied of beauties, the gift

Of your small breath, the drenched grass
Smell of your sleeps, lilies, lilies.

Their flesh bears no relation.
Cold folds of ego, the calla,

And the tiger, embellishing itself ——
Spots, and a spread of hot petals.

The comets
Have such a space to cross.

Such coldness, forgetfulness.
So your gestures flake off ——

Warm and human, then their pink light
Bleeding and peeling

Through the black amnesias of heaven.
Why am I given

These lamps, these planets
Failing like blessings, like flakes

Six-sided, white
On my eyes, my lips, my hair

Touching and melting.
Nowhere.

THIS IS JUST TO SAY

William Carlos Williams

I have eaten
the plums
that were in
the icebox

and which
you were probably
saving
for breakfast

Forgive me
they were delicious
so sweet
and so cold

WHICH RECOUNTS HOW FANTASY CONTENTS ITSELF WITH HONORABLE LOVE

Sor Juana Inés de la Cruz

Stay, shadow of contentment too short-lived,
illusion of enchantment I most prize,
fair image for whom happily I die,
sweet fiction for whom painfully I live.

If answering your charms' imperative,
compliant, I like steel to magnet fly,
by what logic do you flatter and entice,
only to flee, a taunting fugitive?

'Tis no triumph that you so smugly boast
that I fell victim to your tyranny;
though from encircling bonds that held you fast

your elusive form too readily slipped free,
and though to my arms you are forever lost,
you are a prisoner in my fantasy.

translated by Margaret Sayers Peden

anyone lived in a pretty how town

e. e. cummings

anyone lived in a pretty how town
(with up so floating many bells down)
spring summer autumn winter
he sang his didn't he danced his did.

Women and men(both little and small)
cared for anyone not at all
they sowed their isn't they reaped their same
sun moon stars rain

children guessed(but only a few
and down they forgot as up they grew
autumn winter spring summer)
that noone loved him more by more

when by now and tree by leaf
she laughed his joy she cried his grief
bird by snow and stir by still
anyone's any was all to her

someones married their everyones
laughed their cryings and did their dance
(sleep wake hope and then)they
said their nevers they slept their dream

stars rain sun moon
(and only the snow can begin to explain
how children are apt to forget to remember
with up so floating many bells down)

one day anyone died i guess
(and noone stooped to kiss his face)
busy folk buried them side by side
little by little and was by was

all by all and deep by deep
and more by more they dream their sleep
noone and anyone earth by april
wish by spirit and if by yes.

Women and men(both dong and ding)
summer autumn winter spring
reaped their sowing and went their came
sun moon stars rain

DULCE ET DECORUM EST

Wilfred Owen

Bent double, like old beggars under sacks,
Knock-kneed, coughing like hags, we cursed through
        sludge,
Till on the haunting flares we turned our backs
And towards our distant rest began to trudge.
Men marched asleep. Many had lost their boots
But limped on, blood-shod. All went lame; all blind;
Drunk with fatigue; deaf even to the hoots
Of tired, outstripped Five-Nines that dropped behind.

Gas! Gas! Quick, boys! — An ecstasy of fumbling,
Fitting the clumsy helmets just in time;
But someone still was yelling out and stumbling
And flound'ring like a man in fire or lime . . .
Dim, through the misty panes and thick green light,
As under a green sea, I saw him drowning.
In all my dreams, before my helpless sight,
He plunges at me, guttering, choking, drowning.

If in some smothering dreams you too could pace
Behind the wagon that we flung him in,
And watch the white eyes writhing in his face,
His hanging face, like a devil's sick of sin;

If you could hear, at every jolt, the blood
Come gargling from the froth-corrupted lungs,
Obscene as cancer, bitter as the cud
Of vile, incurable sores on innocent tongues, —
My friend, you would not tell with such high zest
To children ardent for some desperate glory,
The old Lie: Dulce et decorum est
Pro patria mori.

(UNTITLED)

Emily Dickinson

My Life had stood–a Loaded Gun–
In Corners–till a Day
The Owner passed–identified–
And carried Me away–

And now We roam in Sovereign Woods–
And now We hunt the Doe–
And every time I speak for Him–
The Mountains straight reply–

And do I smile, such cordial light
Upon the Valley glow–
It is as a Vesuvian face
Had let its pleasure through–

And when at Night–Our good Day done–
I guard My Master's Head–
'Tis better than the Eider-Duck's
Deep Pillow–to have shared–

To foe of His–I'm deadly foe–
None stir the second time–
On whom I lay a Yellow Eye–
Or an emphatic Thumb–

Though I than He–may longer live
He longer must–than I–
For I have but the power to kill,
Without–the power to die–

ARCHAIC TORSO OF APOLLO

Rainer Maria Rilke

We cannot know his legendary head
with eyes like ripening fruit. And yet his torso
is still suffused with brilliance from inside,
like a lamp, in which his gaze, now turned to low,

gleams in all its power. Otherwise
the curved breast could not dazzle you so, nor could
a smile run through the placid hips and thighs
to that dark center where procreation flared.

Otherwise this stone would seem defaced
beneath the translucent cascade of the shoulders
and would not glisten like a wild beast's fur:

would not, from all the borders of itself,
burst like a star: for here there is no place
that does not see you. You must change your life.

translated by Stephen Mitchell

TO S. M., A YOUNG AFRICAN PAINTER, ON SEEING HIS WORKS.

Phillis Wheatley

To show the lab'ring bosom's deep intent,
And thought in living characters to paint,
When first thy pencil did those beauties give,
And breathing figures learnt from thee to live,
How did those prospects give my soul delight,
A new creation rushing on my sight?
Still, wond'rous youth! each noble path pursue,
On deathless glories fix thine ardent view:
Still may the painter's and the poet's fire
To aid thy pencil, and thy verse conspire!
And may the charms of each seraphic theme
Conduct thy footsteps to immortal fame!
High to the blissful wonders of the skies
Elate thy soul, and raise thy wishful eyes.
Thrice happy, when exalted to survey
That splendid city, crown'd with endless day,
Whose twice six gates on radiant hinges ring:
Celestal *Salem* blooms in endless spring.

Calm and serene thy moments glide along,
And may the muse inspire each future song!
Still, with the sweets of contemplation bless'd,

May peace with balmy wings your soul invest!
But when these shades of time are chas'd away,
And darkness ends in everlasting day,
On what seraphic pinions shall we move,
And view the landscapes in the realms above?
There shall thy tongue in heav'nly murmurs flow,
And there my muse with heav'nly transport glow:
No more to tell of *Damon's* tender sighs,
Or rising radiance of *Aurora's* eyes,
For nobler themes demand a nobler strain,
And purer language on th' ethereal plain.
Cease, gentle muse! the solemn gloom of night
Now seals the fair creation from my sight.

from TRILOGY:
THE WALLS DO NOT FALL

H.D.

Yet we, the latter-day twice-born,
have our bad moments when

dragging the forlorn
husk of self after us,

we are forced to confess to
malaise and embarrassment;

we pull at this dead shell,
struggle but we must wait

till the new Sun dries off
the old-body humours;

awkwardly, we drag this stale
old will, old volition, old habit

about with us;
we are these people,

wistful, ironical, wilful,
who have no part in

new-world reconstruction,
in the confederacy of labour,

the practical issues of art
and the cataloguing of utilities:

O, do not look up
into the air,

you who are occupied
in the bewildering

sand-heap maze
of present-day endeavour;

you will be, not so much frightened
as paralysed with inaction,

and anyhow,
we have not crawled so very far

up our individual grass-blade
toward our individual star.

JABBERWOCKY

Lewis Carroll

'Twas brillig, and the slithy toves
   Did gyre and gimble in the wabe:
All mimsy were the borogoves,
   And the mome raths outgrabe.

"Beware the Jabberwock, my son!
   The jaws that bite, the claws that catch!
Beware the Jubjub bird, and shun
   The frumious Bandersnatch!"

He took his vorpal sword in hand:
   Long time the manxome foe he sought —
So rested he by the Tumtum tree,
   And stood awhile in thought.

And, as in uffish thought he stood,
   The Jabberwock, with eyes of flame,
Came whiffling through the tulgey wood,
   And burbled as it came!

One, two! One, two! And through and through
   The vorpal blade went snicker-snack!

He left it dead, and with its head
  He went galumphing back.

"And hast thou slain the Jabberwock?
  Come to my arms, my beamish boy!
O frabjous day! Callooh! Callay!"
  He chortled in his joy.

'Twas brillig, and the slithy toves
  Did gyre and gimble in the wabe:
All mimsy were the borogoves,
  And the mome raths outgrabe.

THE TYGER

William Blake

Tyger! Tyger! burning bright
In the forests of the night,
What immortal hand or eye
Could frame thy fearful symmetry?

In what distant deeps or skies
Burnt the fire of thine eyes?
On what wings dare he aspire?
What the hand dare seize the fire?

And what shoulder, and what art,
Could twist the sinews of thy heart?
And when thy heart began to beat,
What dread hand? and what dread feet?

What the hammer? what the chain?
In what furnace was thy brain?
What the anvil? what dread grasp
Dare its deadly terrors clasp?

When the stars threw down their spears
And watered heaven with their tears,

Did he smile his work to see?
Did he who made the Lamb make thee?

Tyger! Tyger! burning bright
In the forests of the night,
What immortal hand or eye
Dare frame thy fearful symmetry?

MOTHER TO SON

Langston Hughes

Well, son, I'll tell you:
Life for me ain't been no crystal stair.
It's had tacks in it,
And splinters,
And boards torn up,
And places with no carpet on the floor —
Bare.
But all the time
I'se been a-climbin' on,
And reachin' landin's,
And turnin' corners,
And sometimes goin' in the dark
Where there ain't been no light.
So boy, don't you turn back.
Don't you set down on the steps
'Cause you finds it's kinder hard.
Don't you fall now —
For I'se still goin', honey,
I'se still climbin',
And life for me ain't been no crystal stair.

EASTER WINGS

George Herbert

Lord, who createdst man in wealth and store,
Though foolishly he lost the same,
Decaying more and more
Till he became
Most poor:
With Thee
O let me rise
As larks, harmoniously,
And sing this day Thy victories:
Then shall the fall further the flight in me.

My tender age in sorrow did begin:
And still with sicknesses and shame
Thou did'st so punish sin,
That I became
Most thin.
With thee
Let me combine
And feel thy victory:
For, if I imp my wing on thine,
Affliction shall advance the flight in me.

THE ROAD NOT TAKEN

Robert Frost

Two roads diverged in a yellow wood,
And sorry I could not travel both
And be one traveler, long I stood
And looked down one as far as I could
To where it bent in the undergrowth;

Then took the other, as just as fair,
And having perhaps the better claim,
Because it was grassy and wanted wear;
Though as for that, the passing there
Had worn them really about the same,

And both that morning equally lay
In leaves no step had trodden black.
Oh, I kept the first for another day!
Yet knowing how way leads on to way,
I doubted if I should ever come back.

I shall be telling this with a sigh
Somewhere ages and ages hence:
Two roads diverged in a wood, and I —
I took the one less traveled by,
And that has made all the difference.

THE TRIPLE FOOL

John Donne

I am two fools, I know,
  For loving, and for saying so
    In whining poetry;
But where's that wise man, that would not be I,
    If she would not deny?
Then as th' earth's inward narrow crooked lanes
  Do purge sea water's fretful salt away,
I thought, if I could draw my pains
  Through rhyme's vexation, I should them allay.
Grief brought to numbers cannot be so fierce,
For he tames it, that fetters it in verse.

But when I have done so,
  Some man, his art and voice to show,
    Doth set and sing my pain;
And, by delighting many, frees again
    Grief, which verse did restrain.
To love and grief tribute of verse belongs,
  But not of such as pleases when 'tis read.
Both are increasèd by such songs,
  For both their triumphs so are published,
And I, which was two fools, do so grow three.
Who are a little wise, the best fools be.

REMEMBRANCE

Emily Brontë

Cold in the earth — and the deep snow piled above thee,
Far, far removed, cold in the dreary grave!
Have I forgot, my only Love, to love thee,
Severed at last by Time's all-severing wave?

Now, when alone, do my thoughts no longer hover
Over the mountains, on that northern shore,
Resting their wings where heath and fern-leaves cover
That noble heart for ever, ever more?

Cold in the earth — and fifteen wild Decembers
From those brown hills, have melted into spring —
Faithful indeed is the spirit that remembers
After such years of change and suffering!

Sweet Love of youth, forgive if I forget thee,
While the world's tide is bearing me along:
Other desires and darker hopes beset me,
Hopes which obscure, but cannot do thee wrong!

No later light has lightened up my heaven;
No second morn has ever shone for me:

All my life's bliss from thy dear life was given —
All my life's bliss is in the grave with thee.

But, when the days of golden dreams had perished,
And even Despair was powerless to destroy,
Then did I learn how existence could be cherished,
Strengthened, and fed without the aid of joy;

Then did I check the tears of useless passion,
Weaned my young soul from yearning after thine;
Sternly denied its burning wish to hasten
Down to that tomb already more than mine!

And, even yet, I dare not let it languish,
Dare not indulge in memory's rapturous pain;
Once drinking deep of that divinest anguish,
How could I seek the empty world again?

THE BEAN EATERS

Gwendolyn Brooks

They eat beans mostly, this old yellow pair.
Dinner is a casual affair.
Plain chipware on a plain and creaking wood,
Tin flatware.

Two who are Mostly Good.
Two who have lived their day,
But keep on putting on their clothes
And putting things away.

And remembering . . .
Remembering, with twinklings and twinges,
As they lean over the beans in their rented back room that
      is full of beads and receipts and dolls and cloths,
      tobacco crumbs, vases and fringes.

THIRTEEN WAYS OF LOOKING AT A BLACKBIRD

Wallace Stevens

1
Among twenty snowy mountains,
The only moving thing
Was the eye of the blackbird.

2
I was of three minds,
Like a tree
In which there are three blackbirds.

3
The blackbird whirled in the autumn winds.
It was a small part of the pantomime.

4
A man and a woman
Are one.
A man and a woman and a blackbird
Are one.

5
I do not know which to prefer,
The beauty of inflections
Or the beauty of innuendoes,

The blackbird whistling
Or just after.

6
Icicles filled the long window
With barbaric glass.
The shadow of the blackbird
Crossed it, to and fro.
The mood
Traced in the shadow
An indecipherable cause.

7
O thin men of Haddam,
Why do you imagine golden birds?
Do you not see how the blackbird
Walks around the feet
Of the women about you?

8
I know noble accents
And lucid, inescapable rhythms;
But I know, too,
That the blackbird is involved
In what I know.

9
When the blackbird flew out of sight,
It marked the edge
Of one of many circles.

10
At the sight of blackbirds
Flying in a green light,
Even the bawds of euphony
Would cry out sharply.

11
He rode over Connecticut
In a glass coach.
Once, a fear pierced him,
In that he mistook
The shadow of his equipage
For blackbirds.

12
The river is moving.
The blackbird must be flying.

13
It was evening all afternoon.
It was snowing
And it was going to snow.
The blackbird sat
In the cedar-limbs.

THE WOODSPURGE

Dante Gabriel Rossetti

The wind flapped loose, the wind was still,
Shaken out dead from tree and hill:
I had walked on at the wind's will, —
I sat now, for the wind was still.

Between my knees my forehead was, —
My lips, drawn in, said not Alas!
My hair was over in the grass,
My naked ears heard the day pass.

My eyes, wide open, had the run
Of some ten weeds to fix upon;
Among those few, out of the sun,
The woodspurge flowered, three cups in one.

From perfect grief there need not be
Wisdom or even memory:
One thing then learnt remains to me, —
The woodspurge has a cup of three.

STORYTELLING

Barbara Guest

            (introduce pavement)
Old-fashioned people in clothes.

Passage to friendship   *(details,momentum.firefly)*
   wave "bye bye,"

idly unfolds.

          (dark,light,etc.)

          (separately, form,)

    indifferent combinations. *(jest,tears.)*

(*Rhythm   upswing)* (collision with serpent),

          repeat and repeat moonlight
            as suspense, moonlight.

DELIGHT IN DISORDER

Robert Herrick

A sweet disorder in the dress
Kindles in clothes a wantonness.
A lawn about the shoulders thrown
Into a fine distractión;
An erring lace, which here and there
Enthralls the crimson stomacher;
A cuff neglectful, and thereby
Ribbons to flow confusèdly;
A winning wave, deserving note,
In the tempestuous petticoat;
A careless shoestring, in whose tie
I see a wild civility;
Do more bewitch me than when art
Is too precise in every part.

WHO HAS SEEN THE WIND?

Christina Georgina Rossetti

Who has seen the wind?
    Neither I nor you:
But when the leaves hang trembling,
    The wind is passing through.

Who has seen the wind?
    Neither you nor I:
But when the trees bow down their heads,
    The wind is passing by.

TRAVEL

Edna St. Vincent Millay

The railroad track is miles away,
   And the day is loud with voices speaking,
Yet there isn't a train goes by all day
   But I hear its whistle shrieking.

All night there isn't a train goes by,
   Though the night is still for sleep and dreaming,
But I see its cinders red on the sky,
   And hear its engine steaming.

My heart is warm with the friends I make,
   And better friends I'll not be knowing;
Yet there isn't a train I wouldn't take,
   No matter where it's going.

THE DOUBT OF FUTURE FOES

Elizabeth I

The doubt of future foes exiles my present joy,
And wit me warns to shun such snares as threaten mine
    annoy.
For falsehood now doth flow and subject faith doth ebb,
Which would not be if reason ruled or wisdom weaved
    the web.
But clouds of toys untried do cloak aspiring minds,
Which turn to rain of late repent by course of changèd
    winds.
The top of hope supposed, the root of ruth will be,
And fruitless all their grassèd guiles, as shortly ye shall see.
The dazzled eyes with pride, which great ambition blinds,
Shall be unsealed by worthy wights whose foresight
    falsehood finds.

The daughter of debate that eke discord doth sow,
Shall reap no gain where former rule hath taught still
    peace to grow.
No foreign banished wight shall anchor in this port;
Our realm it brooks no stranger's force, let them
    elsewhere resort.
Our rusty sword with rest shall first his edge employ
To poll the tops that seek such change and gape for joy.

TENEBRIS

Angelina Weld Grimké

There is a tree, by day,
That, at night,
Has a shadow,
A hand huge and black,
With fingers long and black.
    All through the dark,
Against the white man's house,
    In the little wind,
The black hand plucks and plucks
    At the bricks.
The bricks are the color of blood and very small.
    Is it a black hand,
    Or is it a shadow?

DO NOT GO GENTLE
INTO THAT GOOD NIGHT

Dylan Thomas

Do not go gentle into that good night,
Old age should burn and rave at close of day;
Rage, rage against the dying of the light.

Though wise men at their end know dark is right,
Because their words had forked no lightning they
Do not go gentle into that good night.

Good men, the last wave by, crying how bright
Their frail deeds might have danced in a green bay,
Rage, rage against the dying of the light.

Wild men who caught and sang the sun in flight,
And learn, too late, they grieved it on its way,
Do not go gentle into that good night.

Grave men, near death, who see with blinding sight
Blind eyes could blaze like meteors and be gay,
Rage, rage against the dying of the light.

And you, my father, there on the sad height,
Curse, bless, me now with your fierce tears, I pray.
Do not go gentle into that good night.
Rage, rage against the dying of the light.

SONNET 43

Elizabeth Barrett Browning

How do I love thee? Let me count the ways.
I love thee to the depth and breadth and height
My soul can reach, when feeling out of sight
For the ends of Being and ideal Grace.
I love thee to the level of everyday's
Most quiet need, by sun and candle-light.
I love thee freely, as men strive for Right;
I love thee purely, as they turn from Praise.
I love thee with the passion put to use
In my old griefs, and with my childhood's faith,
I love thee with a love I seemed to lose
With my lost saints — I love thee with the breath,
Smiles, tears, of all my life — and, if God choose,
I shall but love thee better after death.

DOVER BEACH

Matthew Arnold

The sea is calm tonight.
The tide is full, the moon lies fair
Upon the straits; on the French coast the light
Gleams and is gone; the cliffs of England stand,
Glimmering and vast, out in the tranquil bay.
Come to the window, sweet is the night-air!
Only, from the long line of spray
Where the sea meets the moon-blanched land,
Listen! you hear the grating roar
Of pebbles which the waves draw back, and fling,
At their return, up the high strand,
Begin, and cease, and then again begin,
With tremulous cadence slow, and bring
The eternal note of sadness in.

Sophocles long ago
Heard it on the Aegean, and it brought
Into his mind the turbid ebb and flow
Of human misery; we
Find also in the sound a thought,
Hearing it by this distant northern sea.

The Sea of Faith
Was once, too, at the full, and round earth's shore

Lay like the folds of a bright girdle furled.
But now I only hear
Its melancholy, long, withdrawing roar,
Retreating, to the breath
Of the night-wind, down the vast edges drear
And naked shingles of the world.

Ah, love, let us be true
To one another! for the world, which seems
To lie before us like a land of dreams,
So various, so beautiful, so new,
Hath really neither joy, nor love, nor light,
Nor certitude, nor peace, nor help for pain;
And we are here as on a darkling plain
Swept with confused alarms of struggle and flight,
Where ignorant armies clash by night.

I MAY, I MIGHT, I MUST

Marianne Moore

If you will tell me why the fen
appears impassable, I then
will tell you why I think that I
can get across it if I try.

POETS TO COME

Walt Whitman

Poets to come! orators, singers, musicians to come!
Not to-day is to justify me and answer what I am for,
But you, a new brood, native, athletic, continental,
    greater than before known,
Arouse! for you must justify me.
I myself but write one or two indicative words for the
    future,
I but advance a moment only to wheel and hurry back
    in the darkness.

I am a man who, sauntering along without fully
    stopping, turns a casual look upon you and then
    averts his face,
Leaving it to you to prove and define it,
Expecting the main things from you.

PERMISSIONS